Daddy's Colouring Book...
...and mine too!

I ♡ colouring with Daddy

J. McCormick and C. McCormick

All rights reserved. No part of this publication may be reproduced in whole or in part, stored in any retrieval system, or transmitted in any form or by any means digitally, electronically, mechanically, by photocopying, by recording, or in any other manner, without prior permission from the author.
All designs copyright J. McCormick and C. McCormick.
First published in 2018.

Colouring Tips

If you place a blank sheet of paper behind the page
you are about to colour, this will ensure
the following page is protected from any marks.

The last pages in the book are blank,
so you can take them out to use as
blotting sheets or colour test pages.

The designs are printed on one side only,
and there are wide margins,
so Daddy can easily cut out pages
for colouring or for display.

Older kids can use a fine line black marker
to add more intricate patterns into the
simpler designs if they like.

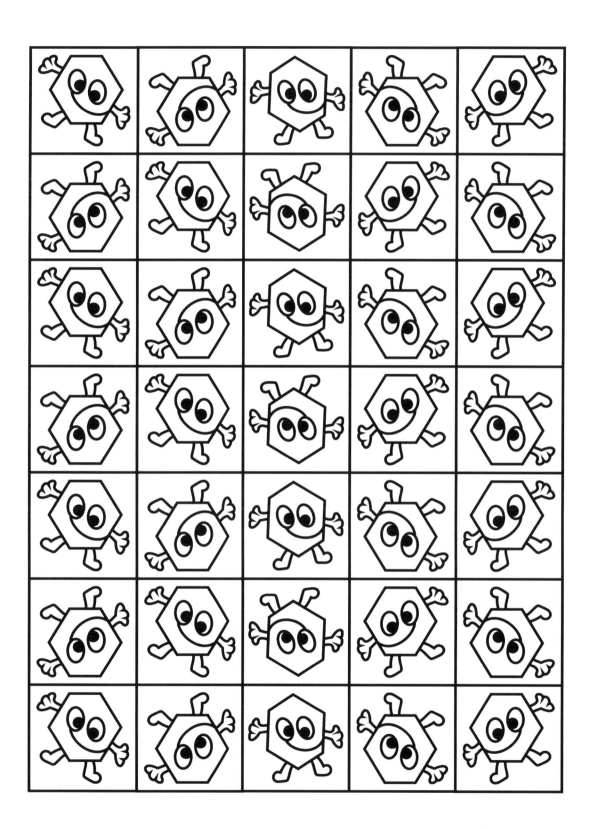

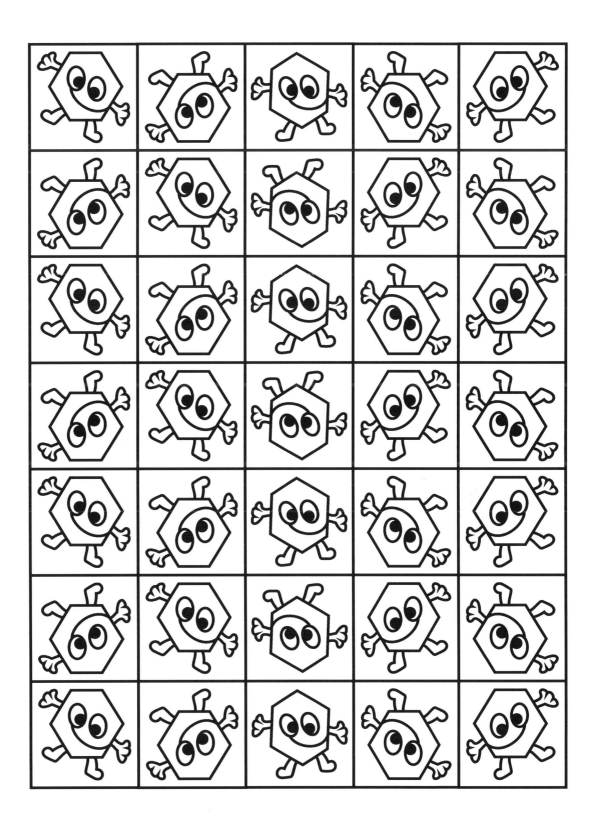

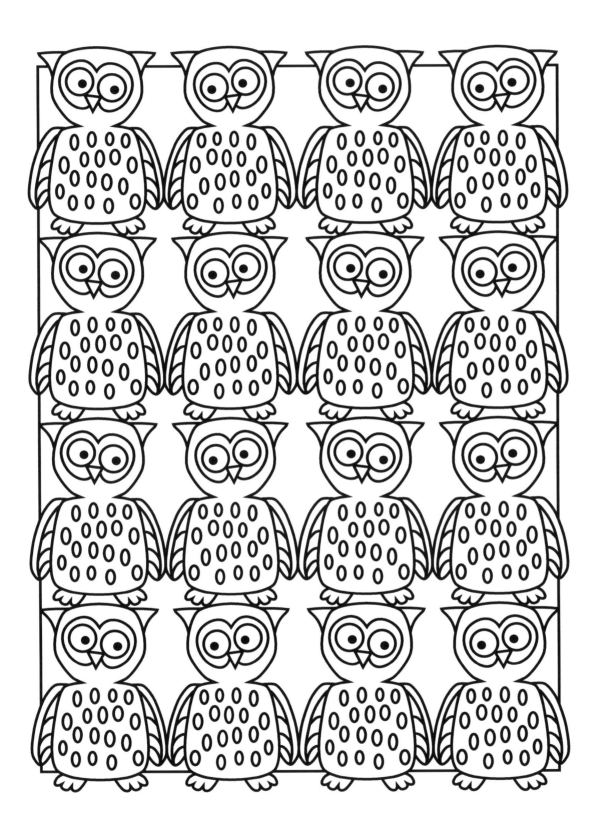

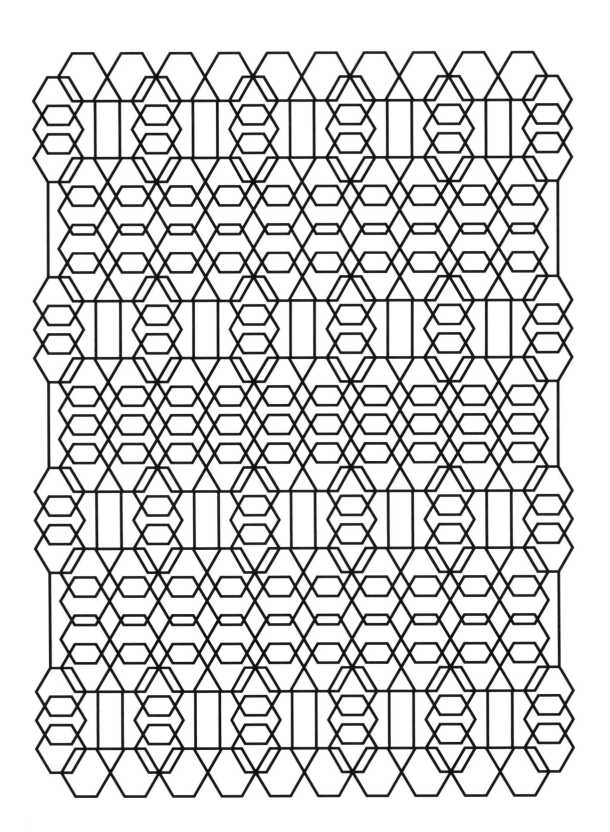

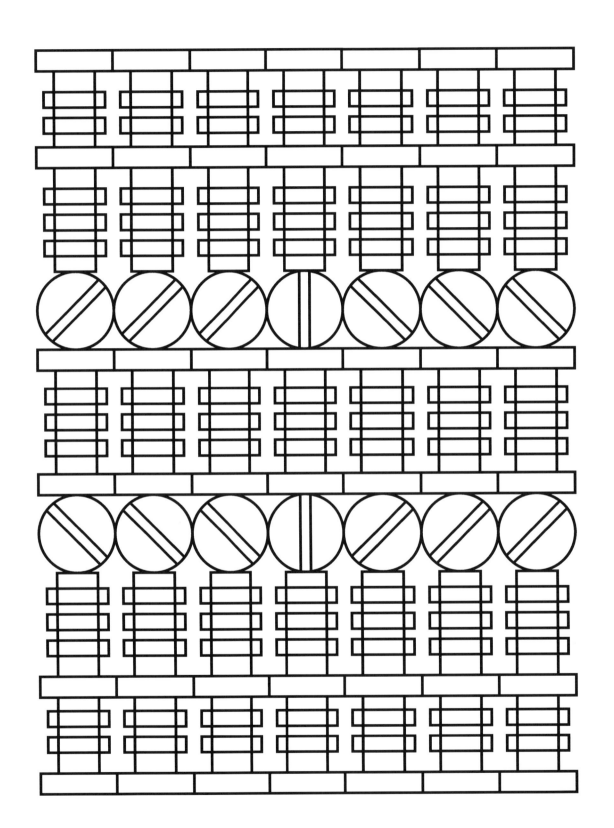

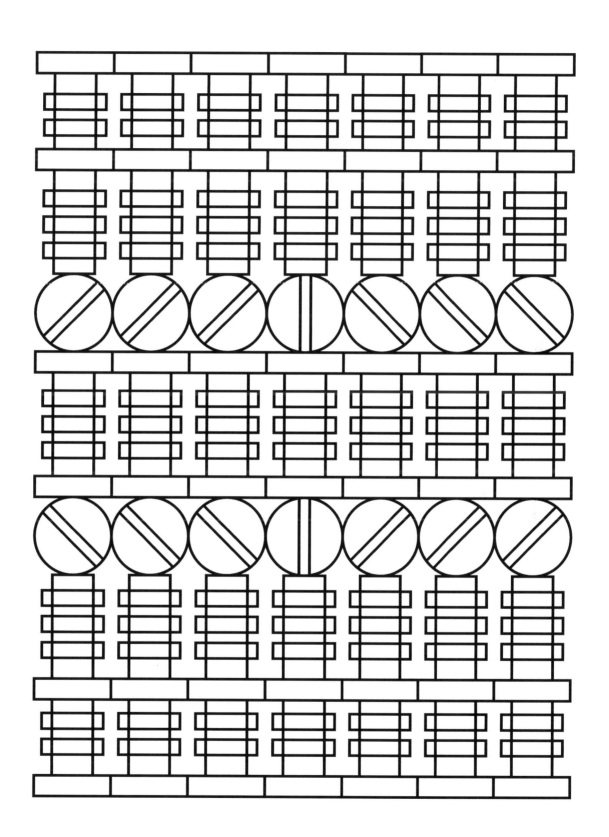

Blotting Sheets or Colour Test Pages

Blotting Sheets or Colour Test Pages

Made in the USA
Lexington, KY
23 August 2019